THE SIDE EFFECTS OF L

Alex Le'Gare

Copyright © 2020 Magesoul Publishing

This is a work of fiction. Names, characters, places, and incidents are a product of the author's imagination. Locales and Public Names are sometimes used for atmospheric purposes. Any resemblance to actual people, living or dead, or to businesses, companies, events, institutions, or locales, is completely coincidental.

Publisher:
Magesoul Publishing
PO Box 580019
BRONX, NY 10458
www.magesoul.com

Editor: Nat White
Book Cover & Internal Format: Adric Ceneri & Nat White
Photography: Alex Le' Gare & Traye Toomer

ISBN: 978-1-953786-00-5

Dedicated To

Tiffany Le Gare

Tiffany, you're the first person
I ever shared any of my poetry with.
We were just little kids then, but your heart was huge,
and your mind was wide for me.

I can't thank you enough.
I wouldn't be me if it weren't for that.

I love you so much. You're the best big Sister in the
world! Thank you for saving my life.

Love always,

Alex

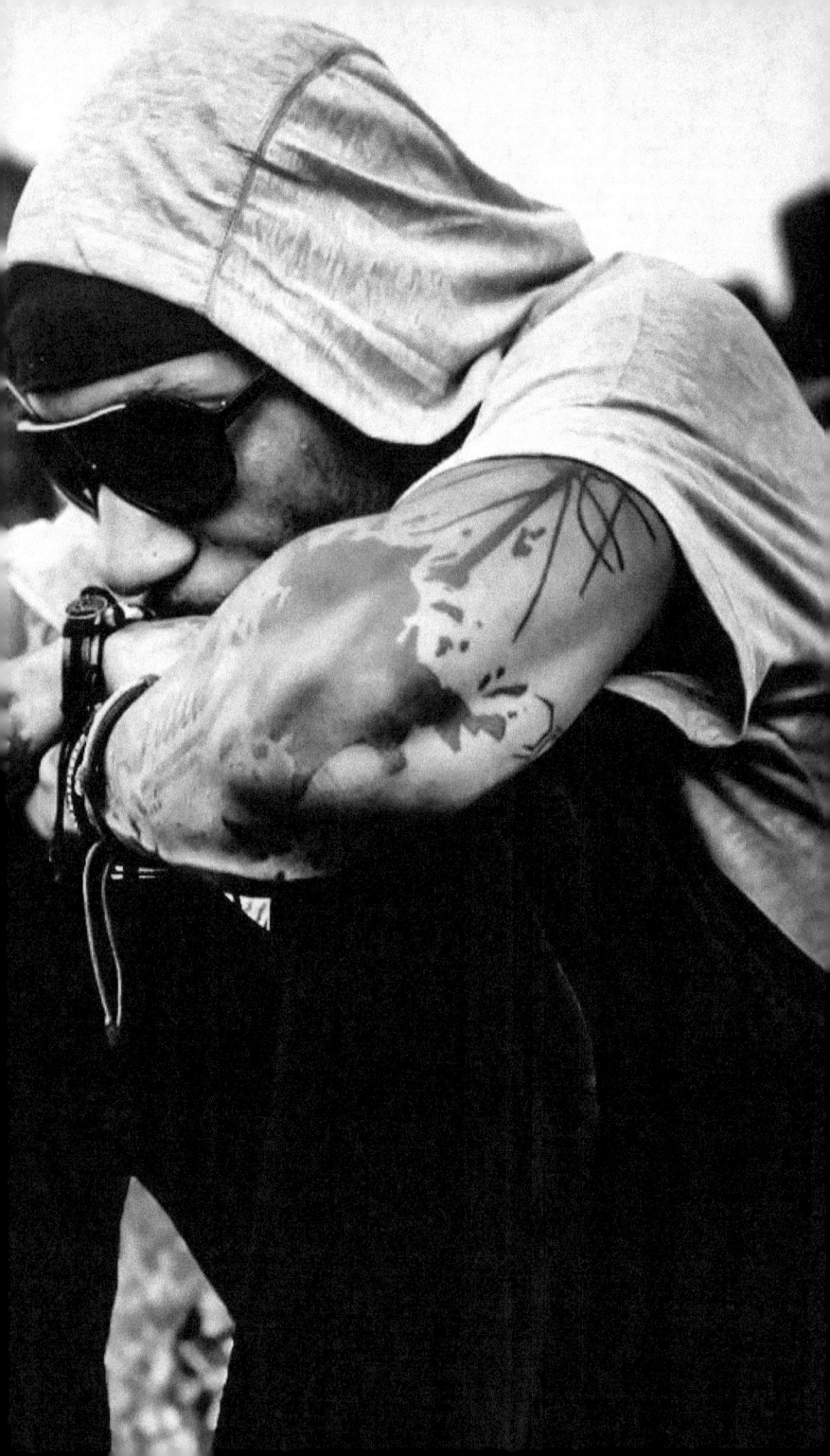

About the Author

Alex (Alexander) Le' Gare is an American Poet from Jacksonville, FL who began reading and writing poetry at the tender age of eight.

Despite having developed a love for literature and art as an adolescent, he would go on to remain a poet in secret for many years, afraid of being misunderstood. However, with a passion for creativity and a desire to inspire poetically; he found himself unable to keep his craft silent and since first performing at age fifteen, he has gone on to share his work via social media outlets and various Poetry Night venues.

Equipped with boundless imagination, paired with a unique sense of rhythm and imagery, Alex delivers his poetry like a painting. Mind-bending metaphors, accompanied by profound simplicity through hints of lyrical storytelling, make his work a unique pleasure to read. Connect with him on Instagram, @alex.legare

Introduction

L is the Roman Numeral symbol of '50'. In numerology, a number's meaning is indicative of its vibrational energy. The law of '5' is expressive of personal freedom, adventure and change, qualities which are all further enhanced when associated with the number '0', which represents the infinite possibilities of the universe. The number '50' expresses a sense of curiosity, variety and spontaneity. Despite an awareness that not everything can be experienced in one lifetime, the idea of trying everything at least once, combined with a desire for progression and growth, results in mastering knowledge through a wide range of experiences. An inquisitive nature drives the passion of this number to explore all life has to offer - embracing diversity, pursuing interests with impulsivity and trialing new concepts in all aspects of life without hesitation nor resistance from its inner self or external influences. The following collection of poems are the side effects of such freedom(s). *

"Mayday"

I pride myself on having met every ghost in this town
Each one showed me less of a sign
Untamed tumbleweeds
blowing in from last time

I played drifter by day
Just so long as by 6 I could kiss my exorcist on the lips
Thanking her
or him
for a split-second friendship

Every alley was painted with apparitions
Some were not my finest work
I could always tell which ones I drew
when I was drunk

In a crawl space called home
I'd light candles
neath a new memento mori
and wait for the sky to break
before I did

My cleanest clothes were saved
Only to be worn whilst visiting graves
Cemeteries look new at night
The mist always seems to accent the trees

I spent the hottest summers in long sleeves
Faith was merely the only thing to ever come up short
A flannel hoodie was a disguise
Without a good enough reason to hide

Francesca was always my favorite
Her corpse was cramped on the crosswalk
She's the last person I ever loved
I thought she'd be harder to recognize
Especially without her eyes

There was never much else to do
other than retaliate
when she took my heart and cracked it
Her body's now target practice

Dead man on the run
in a poltergeist parade
With a V of black swans
as the only source of shade

Nothing was left to hurt or heal
Under the ebony shield of night
I curled up next to the static of voices
who only ever called to say,
"Mayday"

I

WEAR EACH SCAR
AS AN ODE TO YOUR WILL OF SURVIVING
BEFORE YOU INSIST THAT IT'S OKAY TO BE SAD
BE SURE THAT YOU'RE ALL FINISHED CRYING

II

YESTERDAY
SOMEONE SAID THEY WERE PROUD OF ME
AND I SWEAR
IT FELT SWEETER THAN HEARING
"I LOVE YOU"

"Hang 'Em High"

With my thoughts around this throat
I eat my words and choke
So everyone that meets me, now
only get half of what I spoke

While I just sit around with this magic in my neck

Sensitive in my senses
I care just as much
So I feel
Like I'm blinded
Reaching for the epitome
Speaking to the listening
Feeling what's in front
Touching everything
My vicinity is vast

Preaching to the choir is a chore
Some things are meant to be ignored
Love means let go
Everything is retro as soon as it's gone

Vintage with a vengeance

There's always two wrongs
One is never enough
Every vice has its victims
Every killer wants to bluff

Clouds are caged to skies
The Sun goes behind them to die
Each star in my eye is held hostage
Tied together by trance, truths & illusions
Smoke and mirrors; a mirage
They've seen it all, and too much at once
Shoot 'em if they move

III

SLOW MARCH THROUGH THE DARK

SHADOWS EXIST 'CAUSE OF LIGHT

LET THEM FOLLOW US

"Dodging Bullets"

A subtle sigh of relief for my lungs to attest
Sobbing & sorry
I've come to confess
On my lips there's a party
a mumbled-up mess
And it's just getting started
Bending all in one breath

Smell the wind of what I whisper
Catch the scent of what I meant
Wash the remnants you remember
Rinse repentance from my ribs

Take my tongue
it needs a home
away from smoke and tangled truths
Behind my teeth it's been alone
In this mouth, stuck to the roof

So come unwrap the half of me
The part I kept from tragedy
The coroner is mad at me
I should've been a casualty

From the kitchen to the balcony
I crave to counter alchemy
Afraid of what I'm out to eat
Cautious by the faucet

Knowing I'm about to sink

Breathe in, by the exit
I know I've befriended a skeptic
"Goodbye" is a figure of speech
Trapped in line, just between; what's to seek

Surrender your bender in bleach
Allow a new ending to leach
From a screech to a halt in the salt
That very last click in a vault
Dividing the chest to align with a breath
And the only thing left
was ignited in flesh

IV

DID YOU KNOW,
THAT IT'S IMPOSSIBLE TO SURVIVE;
ALL THE WHILE TRYING TO BLEED ENOUGH
FOR SOMEONE ELSE?
IT'S TRUE
BLOOD BEFORE OXYGEN IS BLUE
AS YOUR FACE IS SOON TO BE
UNLESS YOU QUIT HOLDING YOUR BREATH

"The Chewing"

Feel my face with your fingers
Play blind for two seconds
Draw
around my jaw
Brace me biting down
Thump on my throat while I sacrifice saying
Middle fingers on my mouth
A pair of index inside for inspection
I've all my teeth
But my tongue's been half-eaten
by what you can't see

"One Petal at a Time"

Stranger's love
You don't know me
I'm not from around here
I came from out of trees
With glass for leaves
Each autumn--drips my shrapnel
Strips my shade
Spiraling down toward a stay
Reflecting on grounds--
Where I'm resting my roots

V

KEEP THE NEXT MOVE A SECRET

SHIELD IT FROM SHARING

SUCCESS IS YOURS TO KEEP

PROTECT ALL THAT IS POSSIBLE

HAVE A SOLO CELEBRATION IN SILENCE

VI

FAITHLESS FATHERS
MANIC MOTHERS HARD TO HEAL
WE SPAWN FROM REGRET

"Bloodshot, Holy Eyes"

Placed in the old dive diner
By the abandoned Catholic Church
The one with the windows smashed in
and all of the exits burned
Yeah, that one

It always smells like death

But I can't afford to eat
or pay for my sins
So I chill, with an appetite for both
in the barricaded booth near the door
I caught the world in silence
Reaching for the nearest bible
to smash the flies with

Baptized by a barista

Kingdom come by high noon
Beneath the flashing / OPEN / neon sign
As if my halo were electric

"Wake Robin's Witness "
(The Second Eden)

Forgiveness
lied,
fossilized
Planted with the roots of reasons;
to apologize

Carrying on conversations that cut with what sharpened
Our words are the shears
Charged to the overgrown weeds in our facial
expressions
When we cried
Shed were tears of irrigation
We drowned eyelashes down to size
Dragging doubts which weight is of water
Gardening with the tools we found to no use
Chasing each other round the withering; Wake Robin's
witness
Waiting for forgiveness to unearth itself

Why bear the seeds we keep killing
I think we should dig deeper

VII

SACRILEGIOUS SALESMEN
CLEAN UP ON AISLE 4
THERE'RE BODIES ON THE FLOOR
TOO MANY TO IGNORE

"Scarlet Sisters"

In the aftermath of antiquity
Down the center of sight
Where the damage done
Buried up a sleeve,
now home alone; in some heart
Prophesy the promises and proposals
Keep a lie safe from a broken dream
No one needs to see what they won't believe
Offer blank slates and opportunities for buoyance
As time doesn't kindle, it dwindles
Signs aren't simple, nor the people behind them
Pile each child to the tile on the ceiling
Force them from feeling
If it hurts / it's worse / if they smile / it's a signal
Learn to distinguish daddock from durian
Tell the sisters of the scarlet gospel
to only lift their dresses to stretch,
and nurture the nature of our neurosis
To welcome us, with open legs,
and untapped tongues

"Bathtub of Bricks"

We bathed each other in a bathtub of bricks
Bothering bubbles and waking the waters
Washing our battered backs
Wiping welts that felt like welcome mats when rinsed

You show me yours and all you hide
Forgive me if I dive
Won't you hold your breath in mine?
Let's chap lips and give them lines
Mount your mouth along my spine 'til its dry

Bind me to each brick you kiss
Spray paint your spit into what splits
Don't leave me so far as the sink
Seeing as how I could drown by the drain

Be my source of revival
Unashamed, without a towel
Hold it together, not against me
Should you notice that I can't swim

VIII

CHRIST LAID OUT ON THE CROSSWALK

HE LOOKS TOO HOMELESS TO BE NOTICED

SO THE WORLD JUST KEEPS GOING

CRUCIFYING THE CONCRETE

"Purple"

I probably should dismiss you
while my conscience does Jiu-Jitsu
and watch all of the crystals made of pixels flip you
when my lips move

I know I should desert you
But it's like you don't deserve to
find freedom in the creases of the circle
Our heartbeats are purple
It's all so hurtful

Let's not count the chickens
Nor breathe unless they've hatched
Let's hold it in together
Then pretend, it's how we act

You--
My--
Super-intruder
A mind bleak and shaded black
So if you somehow find the entrance
I'll meet you in the back

Watch me flank what's in front
I can double my stunts
One of these things are going to kill me
but not all of them at once

"Layman's Terms"

I don't always follow directions
Sometimes,
signals make me sick to my stomach
Why keep your voice veiled
Don't cradle communication with snide
Rather, kiss my ears with verboten facts
Allow transparencies to travel on, wild
Talk to me and leave traces of treasures I missed
Grant me all of the little things
Feed me tidbits 'til I'm full of a light
But don't gawk if I glow
If your quintessence goes back
to the drawing board
With my attention span dripping in length
Whisper in layman's terms
Leave a soundwave written by woes
Scream unsavory secrets
Be my tutor and learn as you teach
As I've never excelled at reading minds

IX

THE LAST ONE STANDING
WHEN THE CROWD FELL FLAT
HOLDING LOVE BOMBS, PACKED,
WITH A NEW CLEAR VISION
THROUGH A NUCLEAR SENTENCE

"White Flags for Tomorrow"

Another day now drab in the middle of transition
between left and found
Everything looked for was lorn by the last minute
Dusk only douses dawn to cleek
what horizons make new
Which means sunrises are no more
than white flags of surrenderance
from the night before
Creased by crescent moons

Straddled top whatever shade of black that rode my
back 'tween pillars most dodged in the dark

Dismounted by what daybreak drags through distance

Both sides of one sky tied by process of elimination
Inky clouds look a lot like spaces drawn together
Thunder at its thickest
is measured by laps around lightning

One, one thousand
Two, the second coming
Quilting tomorrow in maybes
that'd rather not seem as certain

Pitiless yesterday leaves its mark that much unnoticed
Prying eyes puppify to ylem
While "Goodnight" and, "Good Morning"
became no more than chat to pass everlasting time
with lackluster enthusiasm

Like yesterday found the words to match
the present it kept until now

As if waking up at any given time isn't normal enough
It's just that I've never seen past my palms

X

EVERY SAVIOR NEEDS ITS SHEEP
SACRIFICIAL AND BEHAVING
"FOLLOW ME TO WHERE IT'S STEEP,
I'LL BE SENT TO YOU FOR SAVING"

XI

LIFE IS TATTOOED THROUGH MY NECK
NOT THE WORD, BUT ITS PURPOSE
IT'S SCRATCHED AND IT'S STRETCHED
LIKE THE ARMS I SNATCHED TO THE SURFACE

"Tiger Lily's Revenge"

She keeps her love enclosed
just right beneath her tongue
A taste too rich to waste
Fluent in forgiveness
But knows goodbye in every language

Her smile only occurs once every other ardor
She braids her hair on hardwood floors
Sat in front of a mirror / Indian style
Tiger Lily with the last straw
Only biting whatever's left to chew on

I'll bet you'd like to know when she chokes
Like she'd ever do a thing like that

"*Evaporated Emotions*"

We all should define love
Like when the sky bends its blackness
Twisting tranquility with fists full of hearts
Rinsing out the reddest of requiems
To rain over parades,
and protests
Where puddles are perceived as evaporated
emotions
Just like my daily dose of grace
Where Hail Mary knows her place
See; she shows up in a flash
But never shows up in my face
It's why I've defined love by the grimace in my stare
All these spaces in my eyes
For a witness I should bear
Love is fast
Love is where?
The place you left it, love is there
With a mouth full of mountains
Breathing landscapes aloud
Like a breath of fresh air
Running wild through a child
I've seen pictures in pieces
Been as puzzled as peace--is
Toward a smorgasbord of Lords and cords
Wrapped in faith and forced to war
on each other
out of Love
'til we've seen
another millionth point of view

XII

I WAS MERELY THE WIND
FLOWING THROUGH TIME
SHIFTING THROUGH SPACE
CALMLY THEN FIERCELY, THROUGH THE DAY & NIGHT
LIKE A BREEZY SECRET WEAPON

"Every Skeleton Misses Its Skin"

I sit on a throne made of garbage –
from the mess that I cleaned over time
On my crown are reflections of targets
Every thought that could eat me alive

All my skeletons meshed with the next one
'til they fit in a closet this size
I crept in the room where the elephant loomed
My favorite word is, "nevermind"

I bet the vultures spot me strolling--
on the dead-end side
Circling my steps on the sidewalk
They know I'm dead inside

Love claimed my scalp too long ago
I've borne witness to things blowing up
I kiss the foreheads-- firsthand;
of the ones that hold the guns

Now we mingle in some mansion
In my mind, where I anoint
It's a rendezvous with a toxic view
And even we're besides the point

Stashed in a collection of hugs
I found memories worn to a speck
Somewhere down the line there's enough,
to continue to fly; or eject

In the sky is where I'm left

Until the rain eats my eyes
Waking me alive
While I'm hanging out to dry
Once the Sun doubles back

Just to kill me again

XIII

DOWNLOAD A PURPOSE
FIND FAITH IN THE ENCRYPTION
WE GLITCH IN OUR SLEEP

"Bonnie"

I remember
when she told me about
the gun in her mouth
She said
It blew wind
And bullets in the breeze
I cried
as she died
With my care
in the air
She was a lover
Not built for a widow
With my head out the window
Foot on the gas
We were kissing again

"Clyde"

As if love
is what was driven
Our truth was in the trunk
with our pain
in the ignition
Brown eyes rolled
headlong to black
As good as riddance
of repentance
Buried our hearts
so deep in the road
The only way
that they would come up
is missing

XIV

PENCILING IN

ICONOGRAPHY

LOVE IN HAND BY THE BIBLIOKLEPT

SEDATION IN A SMILE

AN AUTHOR IN AWE

IMAGERY IN ITS WILDEST STATE

THE WRITER IN RAREST FORM

"Photophobia"

Lacking/
Lacking in substance
Roaming through the rubbish
When you're high in public

No one gets it
Shame on them

The city skyline slips
The streetlights are limp
The crosswalks for simps
So I'd rather stay afloat
My shoes are fire, I'm coddled in smoke
However should you stroll, when you're high?

Addicted to art walks and crafty little fixtures
But the scene is always lurking with someone who
wants a picture
So my eyes remain in red
I can't be seen inside the mixture

Less I'm lone and aside
Snapping endless selfies, cause I'm high
With a backdrop in black
A lens focused on what's real
I smile in disguise
Until I'm high enough to feel
Like my vibe is alive sometimes

Whenever I'm alone

"Fireflies & Killing Jars"

It was felt
when she flickered
I watched her eyes
go emerald

We laid in the dirt
And her pupils lit *twice*
with shades
of new grass

This one time
when she touched my face
I felt waves in mid-collision
Been scared to blink
ever since

Fresh from the murk
With stains on her shirt
The crosses she beared
And the ones that she burned

Exhaling an equinox
Each tear its own tantrum
With a fully functional rib cage
to guard all of that damage

We ran laps around a lifeline
Past the point of no response
Resting under willows
Feeding shadows from her light

XV

KILL ME WITH KISSES

LOVE ME TO DEATH

XVI

FORGIVE ME IF I COME OFF STRANGE
I JUST FOUND MYSELF
WANDERING ALONE
AIMLESSLY
LAPPING LABYRINTHS
HEADING HOME
NOT TOO LONG AGO

"The Credit Scroll is My Favorite"

Long walks through the wind
Me, and my plethora of partners
They hold their breaths --
yet --
not my hand.
Never lonely or ostentatious
I like to play the waiting game
Watching them bloom of false sense
Dying to live
Dog eat dog
There's an alcoholic in neglect
A single mother next door
I'll meet them both for the first time, soon
There's just something about being –

INEVITABLE

The scope is roped
Who's ready to be seen / or saved?
Eternity -- it brims
with finicky-less ways -- these days
Always taking whomever
for a stroll
There's a baby with no hope
A horse with broken legs
A bunch of stains
and a human race

I watch them all like a fly on the wall
A universal co-star
to some,
unscripted movie
"But I only eat popcorn at the end."
The Reaper once said

XVII

OFFER EVERYTHING
ASK FOR NOTHING
GET WHAT YOU DESERVE

Sell Your Soul!

CASH 4 SOULS
$5.00

Economics for Children

"The Colors of Care"

Let's start by loosening your grip
Rococo and realism require less pressure
More finesse
Beckon your brush
Busk, yet; with touch
When ten of one's fingers flush
She's bound to the easel you're facing
Creation is crazy
A masterpiece awaiting
To be laminated with the likes of love

Begin at the center
Allow her space to breathe
and take shape
Leaving the corners of the canvas clean
for now
Minimize the mess by stopping when stressed

Stroke a straight line down the middle
Showing, she's of two sides
Acknowledge the divide you've now created
in her mind
Two blanks in one
Fill the first with frustration
The other with fulfillment(s)
Don't force on an image
Try feeling it out

Step back and take it in
See that problems are priced for progression
Know that she's incomplete
Although
Due praise for potential prosperity

Now
dip your brush in her pain and proceed
to outline an outcome
One must
steady each stroke of her struggles

Notice the line that divided now binds
As you've covered the crease
with the *colors of care*

Sensual streaks
The becoming of hair
A flick of the wrist
Splashing at random
Now rapt
Spreads of splatter
A feeling of freedom
Where it lands doesn't matter

Just the sound of it soothes
It's like hearing her laughter
Expressionism ensues

Not to critique what she's become
Rather
to appreciate her allowance
To see her in flashes of satisfaction
Vibrant
and boasting with brightness

From emptiness
With emphasis
on empathy

She's one of a kind
And the globe
is her gallery

"Litterbug"

I saw a piece of paper blowing in the street today
I wondered where it came from
and where it'd end up
It bounced with the breeze,
went wherever wind took it
On a path so crooked, flailing and floating; away

I saw a piece of paper blowing in the street today
Although abandoned and torn
it hadn't lost its form
I'm sure it's seen its share of storms
Withered and worn / softened with age

I saw a piece of paper blowing in the street today
Bent and folded to its destined design
Imperfect, I strained my eyes as it went
Still couldn't make out the lines on its surface

I saw a piece of paper blowing in the street today
Going nowhere in time as it moved
Gracious glimpses of a time it was new
I saw a piece of paper in the street
And it reminded me, of you

Littering love

XVIII

TUCKED AWAY ARE THOUGHTS IN OLD JOURNALS

POWERFUL PROSE & POEMS

CONCEALED WEAPONS, ALL LOADED

WITH TRIGGER WARNINGS

AND FAIRYTALES OF FUNERALS

LOVE STORIES, WITH THE OVERUSE OF WORDS;

LIKE

'BLISS'

'KISS'

AND 'BLEED'

"Wishing on You"

What if it rained enough,
and we woke from some sleep,
to see the sheets of storms flooding the streets;
would we float towards hope—still?

To some pinnacle

Do you think we'd reach a peak, unfound;
without our feet to greet the ground?
What if the raindrops that flooded
were smothered in salt?

Would our eyes then burn at the sight of the Sun?
Would we then squint at the Moon?
What if water ran out of room
and the closest ocean to you was an exit wound?

Where it bleeds
Washing its welts on a beach
So we stand in the sand
and we all hold hands,
telling each other it's fine
But the wind on our friends is the tide coming in

Like gravity grabbing at time

As I'm, never far behind
I'll see you all the time
I'll see you 'til the end
With the rest of the love, I'm to spend

The best of my days where the waves of a current
are drifted in cursive

Signatures of a sea
Penmanship with a purpose

As deep as beginning of Earth is
Though I gaze and I peek toward the surface
Wrapped in the ripple effects of my dive
The top of the waters, my sky

Next one to drown is a shooting star
Should the waves cease to wash away my wish
Before I make it,
on you

XIX

THE HOTTEST SUMMERS
IN THE HEAVIEST OF SWEATERS
STRADDLED BY THE SUN
READY FOR WHATEVER
MISSING YESTERDAY

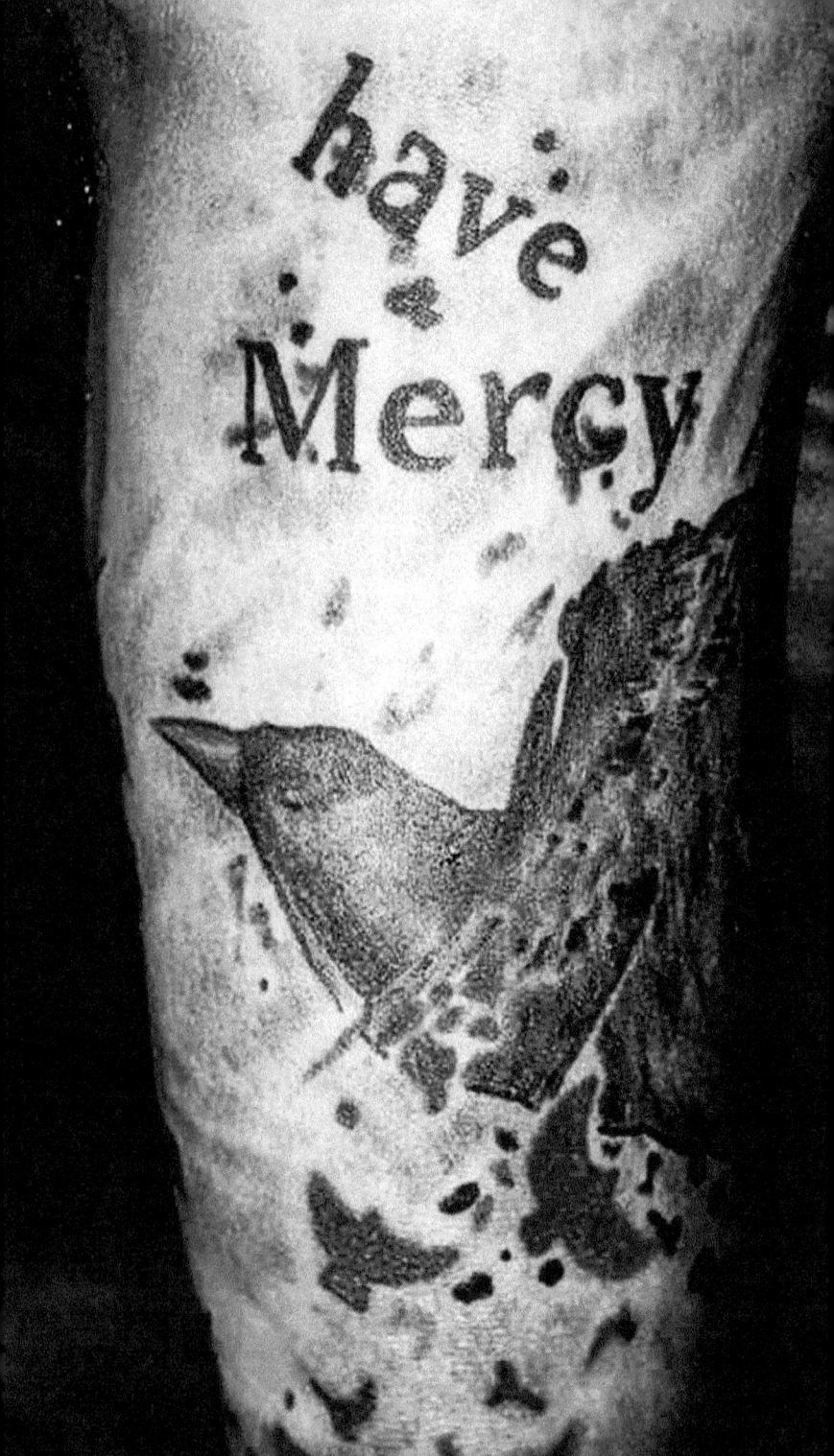

"Strangers"

I want the world to know where I'm headed
I speak to strangers and leave traces of my future
at their feet
I look deep into the eyes of everyone I leave
I trailblaze in a gaze
and keep them not so far behind
My skin
is in overdrive
I reek of rubber, when it burns
I shift gears out of fear
I flash my signals
'til I turn
I beg for pardons
As clarification is an honest craving to pursue
By noon or by night, crouched through
By a woodpeckers waking
Or a night owl's perch
The strangers
smile back at once
Should I choose to smile, first

"Swansong"

She sat softly at the shore like a swan
On the edge of a pond
Measuring my distance
Plotting her path

I'm no more than a drifter
A passer of time
Wound up in the wind
A chaser of chimes

She's uncharted treasure
Sending ripples and relics
Waving me in
The current grows jealous
Whisk me away
Clearly, I'm astray
Here to be gone
We'll never last long

Waters rise when we risk it
Heart taps on tectonics
A wreckage of wanderers
This,
sectoral coquette

Do keep me whole,
for the duration of the devouring
Heterochromia iridium
Her eyes are the shade of her fiery feathers

XX

I WANT TO BLEED ON SHEETS OF PAPER

WON'T DOUBLE-SPACE, MY SOUL TO KEEP

IF I SHOULD DIE FROM BITES OF INERTIA

HEAL MY HEADSTONE WITH A SHARPIE

AND BLEED ON THE BACK

XXI

THE MOON LIES BARE BESIDE ME
HIGHLIGHTING ALL THAT IS SCARRED
AND THOUGH GROTESQUE
THEY'RE ALL THAT GLOW
AND THERE'S THIS VOID IN NIGHT'S LOVE
AND ALL IT'S WORTH IS TEARS
I BATHE IN BEAMS DESPITE THE BURN

"Garden of Statues"

Ever question my thoughts
when I'm staring right at you?
By the mausoleum doors, in the garden of statues
Surrounded and still
A day soon to doom
A love that once bloomed
Now succumbed to some tomb

I turn around to tears, fount
To more backslidden breaths
A snatch giving stretch
to your black ridden dress

Woefully
I'd write
Through wonderstruck waves
and warning signs alike
To go pleading by day
and mourning by night
Beneath August swelter
Attached to all ways
Our pitiful parties
Those depressing soirees

The red of September
October's dead fall
The chills of November
December's last call

With crows through the clouds
Casting shadows of lust
Over Angels and Devils
made of ashes and dust

A pit for the lonely
where love goes to die
Where the ropes of a soul
never mean to untie
As I tug on the cannons
I sip from the vial
Forsaken,
for certain;
in the thick of your smile

Still my pupils grow pale
as I'm staring right at you
My thoughts running rapid
A glare to detach you

I can explain
and keep staring right at you
It's not that I can't
It's that I don't have to

XXII

WRAPPED FEELINGS WITH HER FINGERS

SWITCH THROWN AT MIDNIGHT'S PEAK

A HEART ON HER SLEEVE

BRAINS IN HER HAIR

SCRATCHING THE SURFACE

SPLASHING WARPAINT

EVERYWHERE

"Cloud 9 (am)"

Drugged and drawn out days
Where the sun's rays stayed to play in the pits of your
eyes
As if to dry the cries from last night

Calm, but cranky over coffee
Pass the sugar and the sadness
Let's split the bill and goodbyes
Convinced that it's time
On your wrist is a sign
A casual gaze
As your Casio chimes

Alarming an ending, heard aloud
Excusing me aside, too far away
Take your mouth off mine
Kill the craving of a kiss
Dry your cheeks 'til it's fine

Safe and selfless
Albeit solo
At the settlement of the Sun
Done. You're one. Adrift, in my mind
I've come, to grip what slips and unwinds

Now hitching a ride from some shit in the sky
Call it a cloud
More specifically: 9

Emancipated by an end
Edging along the exodus
Exiting and engulfed in excitement
Elated at the thought of you
erasing me
I encourage all that enlightens you

Peace-like and past whatever's poignant
Where promises placed are played out
And the shade upon the sky rinses regret
While I ride the same cloud that covers you
from being burned again

XXIII

WITH A HEARTBEAT AS QUIET AS A RUMOR
LIKE A SILENCER PRESSED
AGAINST BULLETPROOF FLESH
I KNEW, SHE KEPT HER TREASURES;
IN HER CHEST

"Faceless"

I want to take my face off
But only when you're in it

Trying to transfer the muscles I muster
From the squint in my eye
To that grin on the side
I want to take it off,
so I can see it

I want the chains from my chin
I'll cut the chalk from my cheekbones
From now until more
I want some blood to pour
when I paste my eyes on yours

I can't wait to watch me cringe
When you bend like wind in the balance

My expression / Your escape
Your feelings / My face
Some exit wounds and doors
I look skeptical, I'm sure
Just let me take my bloody face off
and put it on yours

I want to see how it appears
when I'm dining on dust
From the trail of my tongue
to my lips on the loose

I want to see how it looks
when I say how it feels

I want you in my skin
I need you to wear me…

out

XXIV

I FELT HER EVERY TRIGGER

EACH TIME SHE PULLED BACK

I LEANED IN AND BRACED

HER LIPS WERE LIKE GUNS IN MY FACE

"*The Map in Your Mouth*"

Tread like you're trembling
Carefully counter the cracks
Each heart is in a corner
Equipped with strings attached

Confronting ourselves
Each other combined
Somewhere around your spine
You left it all behind

Given just enough time
to tell me it's fine
When every night around 9, I become too far benign
My drinking problem aside
I just need to go outside

And you follow like I swallow
Every bottle on a bottle is hollow
'Til I'm Ichabod Crane
No head, no brain
But my voice is hoarse and you're
Helen at the reigns

A ball and chain that keeps me from gone
How else do we learn
without doing it wrong?

Our favorite song is a seance
This house is an asylum
Every wall is lit with crayon
and handprints we slapped
Hard to hear behind the door,
with your ear against the gap
But if you listened hard enough
you'd resist the urge to *tap,*
or *knock,*
 it *off*

We can run another lap, cause our circle is tight
I bet if we traced it by foot, we could finish by today
No one wants to leave, but they hate to overstay
One of us has to go
"It's better this way."

In your mouth
is a map
and it said so

XXV

CLOCKS ARE CONTROLLED

TIME IS ON THE LOOSE

YOUR EYES ARE FIXED

I'M BROKEN BY SIX

XXVI

THE LAST BREATH IS VISIBLE
COLD AIR ON DISPLAY
I CAN'T FIND THE EXIT
YOU BLOW ME AWAY

"Crosshairs"

Let's pretend you're at your pinnacle
Like your ego is not divisible
I treat problems like a ritual
And you, treat 'em like a task

Going nowhere
So slowly
You only know me 'til it hurts

In an instant
I'm convinced that
your brain is
in reverse

Forward thinking never suits you
So you'll die here
stuck in neutral
I've got a windshield on my pupils
I see through you
far away
Anywhere, I don't care
Tell me where you want to meet me
But the truth is,
you're elusive
And you'd probably never see me

I'm a sniper
I'm not hyper
But my sights are on you

So while you're lost there, in the crosshairs
I'm deciding not to shoot

I was rising to the top
to watch you diving off the roof
I was dying for the truth
But that's like prying out a tooth

See my friends?
I have none
Just a demon
and then some
I can't sleep
'til I lynch one

I need a head beside my bed
I just can't seem to figure
which one

XXVII

MY SMILE'S A NERVOUS TWITCH

THOUGH I'M QUIETLY HEARD THROUGH BRICKS

IF I OPEN MY MOUTH IT'LL BURN MY LIPS

I DEEM SILENCE DEVOUT AND I CHURN MY SPIT

ALL IN AN EFFORT TO CONSERVE THE MIX

"Spit"

You bit your tongue and silence ripped
Scarlet-red spit
I thought you'd soon reveal

Hopeful to heal
Amidst the coming of conclusions
The truth is elusive
Yet
it settles in your saliva

Newfound needs
They hung around like beads
I watched them grow from seeds
After each one was buried by breath

A tapestry
that I tend to transgress
Who said I knew best?
You're the only left
The only one who stayed
Or at least
the only one I kept

Consoling is only constricting
when comfort is cold and conflicting
Swallowing truths lead to spitting

and the consequences claimed their casualties

"Breakfast at Tiffany's"
(the movie)

Misplaced mainstays
Memorabilia left from a muse
All that was stolen was mistook
Keep it in a closet and call it a time capsule
Bury it under the bed with a comforter fit for a coffin
Wipe the windows with old shirts
Watch the way it leaves a kill streak through fog
Listen to the playlists that make a monody of music you
remember them by
Taste the detergent from old clothes just from a scent

Eat breakfast at Tiffany's
And make the booth that the two of you would frequent
some sanctuary
Where comfort never comes on the side
Strangers pass on pavements like elimination of the
lone
Funny you're only complete in a crowd
But can't ever rip the walls of regret
In that one-bedroom apartment

XXVIII

I TRY NOT TO CRY

WHEN I COME TO CONCLUSIONS

BUT MY EYES TEND TO DIE

WHEN I FIND AN ILLUSION

LIKE HINDSIGHT IS FRIED

BUT ALIVE IN CONFUSION

SO MY MIND IS BAPTIZED

IN A TIMELESS SOLUTION

"6"

If I were to have a child
If it were to be a girl
I'd beg permission with a kiss
to love, and name her *6*

Just like the number
No letters to shame
She'd learn how to count
by learning her name

She'd know the 5 before her
and feel the infinite after
But in a world with no reason,
6;
is always even

I'd tell her to raise both her hands
Now really quick
make 2 fists
Then open 1 hand, whichever you choose
And whatever hand is left
lift its index
This means you're whole
to the core
You're a handful
and then some

Everything you hold
and what you have in store
To give all you have
and then a little more

Now keep one hand open, just like your heart
And leave the 1 finger on your other hand arched

Know that you're the second power
of me
So on the count of 3
be you
times 2

Dedicated to my unborn child – 6

XXIX

MAPPING OUT MESSAGES

GRAFFITI GRABBED US

HER AND I DRAWING DAWN ON HIDDEN HORIZONS

NO FAME AND UNNAMED, SCRIBBLING 2 ON THE TRAIN

KISSING IN CURSIVE

CALLIGRAPHY KILLS

"Hangover Hammock"

I was counting my concepts on the countertop
Page by page in the kitchen
A knife near my knuckles
The light was fluorescent and flickered

The fridge neath the freezer was full of my feelings
Even the icemaker shat heart-like shapes
And the eggs grew legs
to crawl
from their carton-esque coffins

I threw an entire series in the sink
It's 20 to 30 pages
I think
My very own devilish delectation
Drowning in dirty dishes

But I was pacing past the pantry
in a panic
PROOF
that the wheels were turning
in mire

Eyes as red as a blood decanter
The tea kettle screams
bloody murder

But,
baby's just high on the hammock
I strolled off the porch
as she perched
My face plants in bloom
cause I'm tired

She whispered goodbye
'til I heard her

XXX

IT'S LIKE THE MOON SAW IT ALL
WHEN THE SUN WAS AWAY
WE SHOT THROUGH THE NIGHT
AND DIED EVERYDAY
LIKE THE STARS
THAT WE ARE

XXXI

I ONCE FOUND GORGEOUSNESS
HANDCUFFED TO A HELM
STEERING STRIPES LIKE STITCHES
ON THE UGLIEST SCARS
LEAVING TRACES THROUGH THE SPACES
NEVER SEEN

"Tsunami"

You were carving out a crevice
Constructing ways to lure
Candleholder with a cure
Coastguard to my conscience

Able of no more
than escape routes to shores
My brainwaves beyond buoy edges

You flare and I follow through salt that I've swallowed
and bottle a message to breathe

Circling sharks in the dark only seen by the spark of
that trigger you tugged

Overboard
Overridden
Overthrown
Unbidden

You claimed you could rescue with love
Now miffed by the drift as your castaway shifts
The crevice you cracked now is plugged

Drowning in depths
Daydreams below deck
Shipwrecked
and up to my neck

What's next?

A lighthouse that's light-years away?
An island an inch from an ending?
Some raft I can't wrap around?
From you?

This,
unnurturing
nautical
nymph

XXXII

I BECAME A VICTIM OF CHEMISTRY

VIBRATIONS AND SUCH

I SOFTENED MYSELF THROUGH SWEETENED SIGHS

AND ANYTHING SAID

SLOWLY

"Tadasana"

Touched by ecru through lilac veins
You'd think that heartbeat broke glass
That marteau -- made whole; on Yoga mats
Elongated exhales of acceptance due to proper
circulation

Otherwise known as, blood flow

Echoes only struggle for existence in silence
Waiting on unspoken octaves to breach upon
Hung by the lashes of time-ridden tongues
Through words relevant by release date

--Reminding one; to grow

But if some mirror takes you down through a place you
left alone
Don't tear your face another hole
Look for fireworks in the burning pupils like a tunnel
with excitement on two ends

Glow, as if not doing so would mean you'd forget how
to by lack of practice
In order to be continued
Meanwhile has to be present at some point
Future locked itself in Tadasana
Stood still like a statue in the reach of eager minds that
stretch aspiration to stitches
Available for aim
So all that ever happens brings it closer
All you have to do is move

"Black"

Today,
I saw God
flesh-bound
We shook hands and hugged
Only to succumb to separate ways

I was granted kisses by the Mrs.
The virgin Mary was scary and mistaken for a lover
But she locked lips with me so much as a whore
Making me one
too

Maybe
Just maybe
That flash of God was me turning wet
Through metaphoric tears I wept
Under stars that kept me as bright as tomorrow

Today
I saw God flesh-bound
with time frozen inside her left thigh,
and so was I;
scared to death

XXXIII

**A VOICE THAT ONLY KEEPS TEMPORARY TRIALS
TIED TOGETHER LIKE TASSELS ROUND A TONGUE**

"The Strength to Sleep"

The one that brings the night's sky down to its purpose
Then kisses me slow through a heap
Just drifted to a dream before hogging all the sheets
I like to watch her sleep
Especially, when she's on her period
because I know the units of the uterus
She's been tested all day
and somehow, she's managed to muscle being
uncomfortable
Somewhere, between tomorrow & yesterday
Without ceasing to amaze, as usual; she finds a way
She falls asleep
ready to deal once more
But first, she'll rest easy
and when she wakes up
I'll be dying
to know
how the fuck she does it

THE SIDE EFFECTS OF L

"Emotional Masochist"

I've said
  "I love you"
and not meant it
I've said
  "I love you too"
and hated myself immediately after the lie
I've been toxic with toxic women
I used to bathe in torture
Seemingly craving it
Knowing that I never planned on forever
with her, or her, or even her
I always knew
that I just needed something to write about;
after we've killed each other

XXXIV

BECAUSE IF YOU LEAVE
I WON'T HAVE ANYTHING TO WRITE ABOUT
EXCEPT YOU...
LEAVING

"Interlude"

Capture it/
Let it go/
Can you feel that?
Go numb/

Does this please you?
Satisfaction/
Denied/
Take it or leave it?
All too hard to decide

Love her/
Crack hearts/
Can she feel that?
Hope not/

Hopeless/
Was she?
In a cage/
Full of traps/

A victim's view/
Through a gap/
The lack of tears/
A vacant lap/

That heavy stench/
As thick as the plot/
An intransigent interlude/
Segway to the end/

"War Torn"

Those flags we picked up
were fully stained
pale ones

Blotched
with the blood
from the battles
that built us

Next to the weapons
that never killed us

Our clothes
look like we've stepped on a landmine

We can't feel
our legs

But it's nice to meet you

XXXV

OLD OAK LIMB
THE ONE I CLUNG TO AS A KID
I NEED YOU IN LIFE'S OCEANS
BUT I'M SURE THAT YOU'RE GORGEOUS, STILL
FORGIVE ME FOR LEAVING YOUR LEAVES,
WITHOUT LEGS WRAPPED 'ROUND THEM
I MISS YOU TOO

XXXVI

PLACES

SWEET PLACES

STRANGE PLACES

PLACES THAT SO RATTLED MY PULSE WITH LIFE

SOMEWHERE THAT DISTANCE IS NO MORE THAN A

DISTRACTION

IF I SHOULD EVER PAY ATTENTION TO THINGS I'VE LEFT

BEHIND

"Wings & Other Frivolous Things"

This sky
is out of space
That's why heaven was erased

And though I'm gone
Through counted days
And calendar stains

Through all is missed

Every scar needs its kiss
Every Angel begs for wings
Amongst a return

and other frivolous things

"Interlude 2"

I was merely the wind
Blowing through time
Sifting through space

Calmly
Turnt fiercely
Through the day and night

Like a breezy secret weapon

The Sun
That was me
I brought closure to clouds

Until half of a Moon
hit you through trees
Shining on streets

I'm at your feet
Guiding you home

XXXVII

BLURRED VISIONS
AN IMPROVEMENT FROM ALL THINGS LEFT BLACK
BUT BLURRY,
NONETHELESS

"The World by its Hair"

I burned everything I ever touched
Guess that's why my palm itches
You'll say, "love you"
I'll say nothing
See how we respond different

You just leave
I branch out
It's like we respawn different

There's a plea within a doubt
And when it breathes
it's long winded

Got the world by its hair
Took it over
like I planned it
Turned dirt to diamonds and gravel to granite
Elongated landscapes
with my palms 'round the planet
Fixed the falsehoods with forgiveness

Scrubbed it clean
I'm heavy-handed

Never hurt much 'til I learned trust
Though real, it's oh so mysterious
How we tend to collide but never combine
You're always curious
I'm always serious

You can hold me 'til it ends
Might as well just say hi to the wind

Love is hell, and it's blind; and it's flawed
So I don't feel
I don't fall
I am no one
like God

XXXVIII

A RED-EYE IN YOUR DIRECTION
DON'T KNOW THE LAST TIME I BLINKED
TOUCHED BY TURBULENCE
PARACHUTES AND PROMISES
BROKEN
WE'VE CUT TIES

"No Such Thing as Nothing"

Incognito on the edge
with a threat to swan dive
Far too young
to pray that it's dead

But I've been doing it for a long time

Engulfing myself in everlasting endings
One of many things
that I often do

Messages mangle the mind in its bending
Far too depressed
Unresponsive
to nudes
Deep fried daydreams
turned food for thought
While lost hand caressed bodies
like braille

For breaths and bite marks
and dirty nails
From scratching on the light bulbs
and switches

Sleek & polished pale

Asleep are the veins of boiling blood
I've blown my brains down to its seams
Fingertips on lips
Blowing off steam

Eyes wide shut
Life is but a dream

XXXIX

CATCH ME IN WHICHEVER ROOM THAT ISN'T SPINNING

HELP ME FINISH PAINTING STOP SIGNS ON THE WALLS

DON'T ASK ABOUT THE WINDOWS

THEY WERE BLACK WHEN I GOT HERE

"Title Be Not"

Sometimes
I cry
As if to liquify my eyes
and hollow myself

Hopeful
the drops won't stop
When drips hit the corners of my lips
and I decide to
swallow myself

The way I weep in my sleep
Strength is stained in these sheets
Should I rinse the drench
and
bottle myself

A subtle puddle
As round as a huddle
Ugly and muddy
And I'm the only one
stomping myself

Just to conquer myself
Like,
all of myself
From the bottom, I felt
It's only been me
Stopping myself

So called obstacles
stealth
In charge of my health
At large is my help
Like I'm God to myself

Too long
since I felt
How strong is that belt?
How new is that noose?

Can I hang out alone,
and get along
by myself?

I've been calm
since I knelt

Though these palms are wet
to welt
I mean,
how else am I supposed to smear
what I've smelt?
Unless I dump the bodies,
I've dealt
On top of myself

Six feet
Skin deep

Wailing
Neath some cryptic collage

Killing the caution
Carving my coffin
Crying to death

All
by myself

"Sleeves"

Let's meet in the smoke
Hold hands
and wave at the haze
Stand our ground and rise above

Lock your eyes with mine
See that you're not that hard to find

Flee furthermore
from the front line

Should I lose you,
move your mask from your mouth
and tell me where you are
Scream
from where it's seemingly safe

I'll come with cupid
Looking with love
On a mission not to miss you

Take cover!
Hide in these sleeves!
I'll help you leave!

Rendezvous with me
under radars

After all
They're shooting at us

XL

NEXT TIME THERE'S A TAP AT THAT DOOR

I'M GOING TO SIT ON THE FLOOR AND STARE AT IT

UNTIL IT STOPS

AND MY FACE SAYS

'DO NOT DISTURB'

XLI

IN A PLACE THAT MY HOME'S NEVER BEEN
FREE AS MOWED GRASS BLADES
FLYING 'ROUND A RADAR;
AND OUT
OF THIS WORLD

"Sundays"

Who cares if it hurts?
All I do is feel anyway
So even if it's pain
I'm sure to ring nostalgia's neck
A brainiac with panic attack
Laid on the backs of blinding breaths

My bed is no more than a chamber
With no life outside of it

Sunday mornings
Minimized outside is the noise
Natures breath on my window
Like a stained-glass vortex
I cried way too hard after drinks
Last night stinks
I can smell it in these sheets
I just want to go back to sleep

They say today is new
So what's yesterday to you
A lesson barely passed
We're lucky if we've learned
anything

I've held the world in my hands
Remote controls turned into phones
Closely connected
and alone
Always slow to get up

Morning breath
The yuck of my yawns
The Sun is as bright as a bomb
And the clouds are paper thin

Where do I begin?

XLII

SHE REJOICED IN A REQUIEM OF ALL THAT SURVIVED

NAKED AND ALIVE

A SIGHT FOR SORE EYES

I JUST HAD TO SEE

"Morticia's Memoir"

Once more,
I gathered the gumption to dance with ghosts
A popularity contest between imaginary friends
Amityville amateurs, all dressed in funeral attire

Broken from earthly approvals,
every girl without a grave came,
to be ostracized accordingly;
to go from victims to vixens
Like phantom fodder

Men and small children, the same

I watched as poltergeists paved the streets of purgatory
Parading 'round their makeshift pentagram
like ornamental orbs
Impassive, yet;
far more lucid than the living

My cold hands have mastered the clockwise motion of
each gas-jet
This ain't my first furnace
Everybody's in the fire

I often danced alone

"Friendly Reminders"

Hold me in the hind of your mind
Where hindsight meets hope
Properly stored
In that notch at the top of the back of your neck
Leave me kept in the rolodex of things
you'll soon remember

Where your spine is connected
At that point behind your jaws
Biting down on the tension
To taste escapes and swallow exits

Settle down in your subconscious

To behold
What blast from the past
nests
then breathes
Where you left it
For future reference

Lay me down behind
your eyelids
Keep a promise
not to peek

So no evil
Look for me
Amidst the ones
that got away

XXLIII

UNVEILED

STRIPPED OF STRIA

VINDICATION OF SKIN BY THE FOOT OF THE BED

TRIUMPHANTLY ALL DONE UP

PROUDLY NUDE

POSING ATOP A PILE OF YESTERDAY'S GARMENTS

"Where I've Been in the Meantime"

There isn't much
if any reason
to tell the tale of whispers
that wrapped me in echoed empathy

After all
those voices ventured vastly throughout
an abyss
Until hidden and hissed

My head
My mind
A minefield of
merry-esque memories
Too often I sought to meddle in

Chasing those echoes
where rosy edges bend
Tracing a threshold
I'd know to never end

What to make of this field?
What's with this paradigmatic paradise
that's been placed at my feet?
These echoes at my ears
Digging through a dream
ripping seams from my sleeves

For peace
Fulfilled promises
Choked by a cold cut breeze

Quietly
Quivering
On que

The slow dust screams
Finally reminding, there's no such thing
If there is
It's out of reach

I can't say to this day that it's parted
But I must admit
I've felt it move

XLIV

DAWNING LASHES FROM LOST LOVE

A FIGUREHEAD OF FORGIVENESS

EAGER ONCE

AGAIN

TO BECKON A BREAKAGE

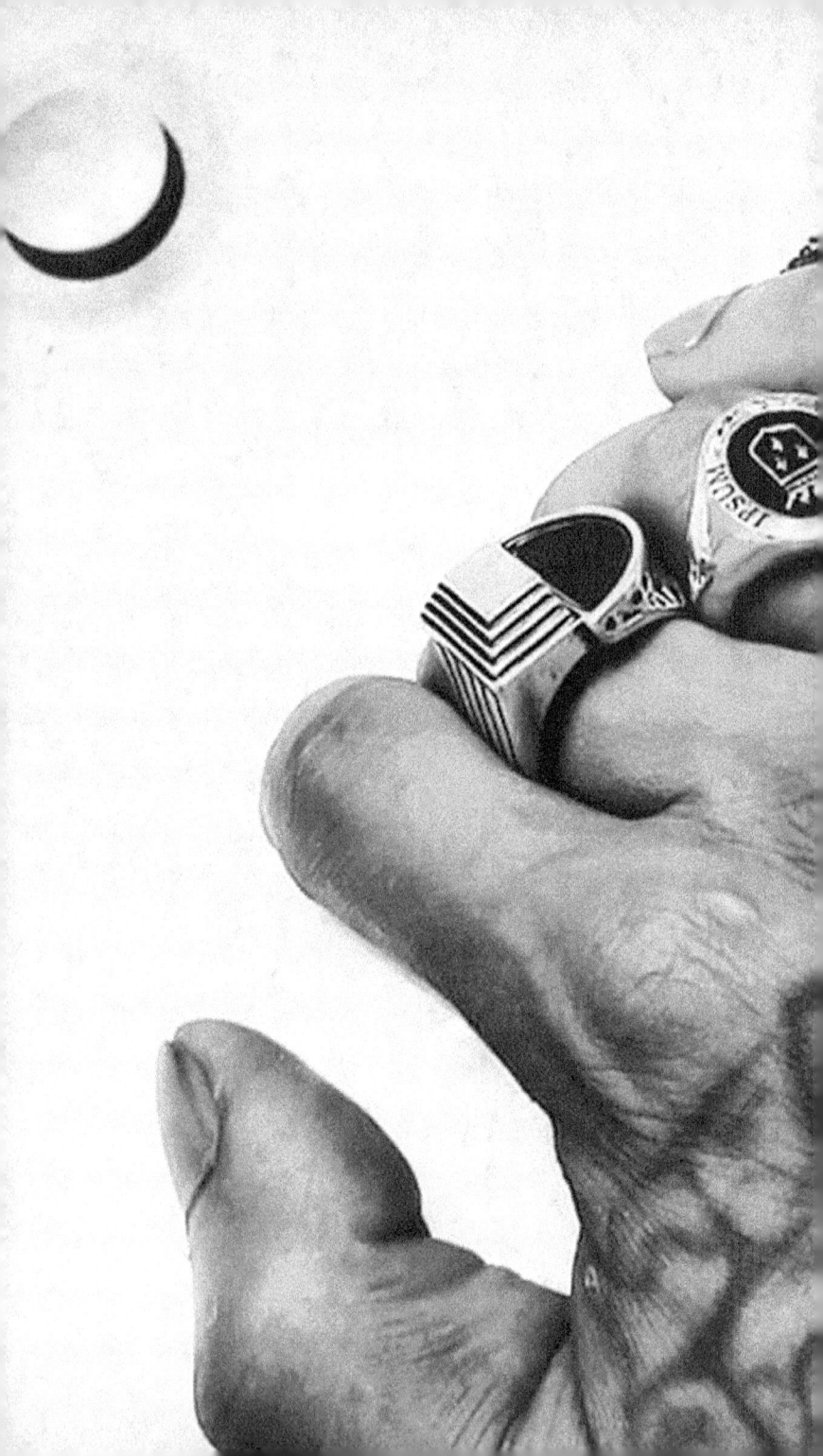

"Etc."

There's a level of suspension
It requires all that is still

You can feel it by the water
If you close your eyes in calm

A river once showed me
Not a ripple was lonely

With my arms to their extent
I slapped space in its face

And once upon an eye shot
Imagination swept me off
No such thing was better
than the water in my eyes

Contemplations
never felt so customary

Killing time
with no more than a caution

To hear the rush of a river
with my face soaking wet

Until clouds came with rain
as if the sky was out to hide

I let it land on my face
and no one knew the difference

Between raindrops and tears

XLV

I ONLY WISH TO BEAR WITNESS UPON EVERYTHING HURTFUL

SEEING AS HOW I'VE NOW NESTLED IN NEGLECTION

TEETERED ON EDGES OF CONSTANT MISUSE

XLVI

BITING MY TONGUE
A MOUTHGUARD OF SILENCE
GRINDING MY TEETH

"Antonella"

So I held your heart in one
Left your mind up for the taking
Should I ever find its depths to pierce
Tell me
when it gets old

We found comfort in the quiet
Pulsating to the wire
Everything was felt aloud
In a labyrinth of silence

I knew nothing more than to breathe
Still air is an exhale
Into my lungs you go
I take you in as my breech

Antonella
I feel you breaking by the ends
Let's hold it together until you say, there's no other way
This is where it gets old
One day you'll have had enough
I don't know which month it's under
But around the corner
Never felt closer

It's an end that's far from over
Beginning with a drag
Us two
came to
heavy healings
What's another bag?

It's just that we hate it
In between those lines
We die in the spaces
Right between the eyes

I can honestly say I saw it coming
Too close for comfort
A windy wil 'o wisp
Was it ever far behind?

Antonella?
Are you listening still?
Are you far too educated
for your listening skills?

Aren't you cramped against that cusp?

There's just enough
pressure
We're both held
in place

Every tear
is an escape route
There's a fire on your face
Day breaks on your matte black brows
Your eyes kill whatever's left

The windows to the soul
Before it bit its way out

O' Antonella
Newness is a virtue
Unaffordable to us
poor souls

All we've got is not enough
There's always each other
Understatements
Overkill

Our tarantella in the balance
Watch me beat my dead heart
Until it gets old
And watch me reign
over
every
regret

"Leftover Senses"

To be wrapped in silence
Quilted & quiet
Deaf
to the subtlest sound of a breath
Need who, say more?
As we grew, pain stored
Blindly
So now you have to feel it to find me

Fingertips strip what's yet to unfurl
Some fingerprints make all the difference in the world
Touching
My skin now moves only due to one's clutching

The scent of a singe makes me cringe
Reminds me of a candle burning at both ends
Smelling
Whose words are now smoky and telling

I've enough amount to bite the bullet
Eating my heart out by breakfast
Tasting
A selection of senses I placed on the table for lovers

And I hate leftovers

XLVII

THEY ALWAYS SAID MY HEAD WAS FILLED WITH NONSENSE

SO I TRIED TO KILL MY THOUGHTS

BUT I ACCIDENTALLY KILLED MY CONSCIENCE

"Star-Vation"

When the stars grow faint
He's welcomed to paint
a labyrinth of question,
so to speak

Leaving only with feelings
Captured and exposed
Waiting for the close
of imagination's toll

Irritated by touch
Groped by the ground
Lying down
Back against the bike lane, brushed by a breeze
Caressed by cars, passing

Days shared with someone's daughter
Naive nights that drowned out danger
Dismissing a dagger, she drew
The slit in her gap is a trap
He, falling victim
The chip on a shoulder is tapped
and she waits behind
Ready to find

The slip in the knot
The seep of raindrops
From the sky when it stops
sunshine's high horse

Crafting a norm
In the eye of a storm
She thought he'd conform
In the rain, she'd detect

But the sighs each plead guilty
to a jury without sound
And he just waits around
...Until she eats the stars

XLVIII

MY HEART KNEW HOW TO BLOCK PEOPLE
BEFORE THERE WAS A BUTTON FOR IT

"Seasons of Sensuality"

It's just that your finger was a little too pretty
When you placed it on my lips
I couldn't help but to
wrap around it

Sort of like your palm
Clouds are made of this material
A silk-like surface that accentuates softness
What a perfect place for my heart

The aim at your wrist
It's as flexible as you are whole
Plus, I can feel your pulse
Should I ever have to save you,
I'm grabbing *here* first

As I rub through your hand
every chill is ignited
Scorching our skin in the name of excitement
Strobes of your strength let me know, as a Poet;
that *this* is the hand that you write with

A scroll up your shoulder
I can tell that you're tense
Not only for now, but in general
Cause I'm feeling a pinch

Your neck rolls around a rub
This soothes you
In the future, I'll place my hand here;
when you're displeased with me

I hope it has the same effect

Stretching through strands of hair to your scalp
Like a victorious Iroquois at war
And by the touch
you opened up

'Twas a ballad, your breathing
That lets me know what you're thinking
What to make of this face?
A relic so rare
Our eyes met again
Growing lost in a stare

We spoke the same language
without ever having to say shit
Your eyes
That's where I'll keep my focus

Oh, but such lips
The surrenderance of a smile
I think I'll mold my mouth there
for a while

With breasts of a beautiful beast
Big enough to be bestowed by a grip
Small enough to require gentle attention
Like mountains of good measure

I long to rest my head here
Should this escapade cease

Just to hear your heart
The beat of all I seek
The hike to an endless peak
From the valley's I've vigorously ventured through

The bottom
to the most organic of organs

So should you say that you love me,
would you please, if you will;
say it from there?

"The Grey"

There's a place called "The Grey"
Surely you've been
There's no middle ground
Just beginning and end
We can't see what's coming
And don't care to know
We just settle in
Filling blanks as we go
No fears when you're here
Numbing is the feel
Pain is a figment
And nothing is for real
Except,
letting go

XLIX

THE BEST THING ABOUT YOU
IS THAT YOU'RE NO BETTER
THAN ANYONE ELSE

"Nebula in a Noose"

What's it like
to die in the sunlight
To be beautifully blinded
Beaten beyond belief

By the biggest and brightest

What's it like
to be placed behind
To die
in the morning

Do you ever find your smile
Does it shine even still

Do you await your return
What's it like when you burn

The night holds you close
A pariah by noon
What's it like
to know you'll be back soon

Time, in all of its essence
leaves your presence at the cusp
Another day is gone
Hence, you sparking over night

What's it like
to claim your place
To sit amidst the glorious glow
To shoot through the sky in a blink

A dance, only held when it's black
What's it like
when the Sun turns it's back
To light the would-be ebony shield called night

What's it like
to know the world only sees you if it stays awake
To resemble some ripples from wrinkles in heaven
Only to be dead
no later than 7
in the morning

L

TO HEAL IS TO BE ALIVE

TO STRIVE IS TO CARRY ON

AS LIFE IS ALWAYS

...TO BE CONTINUED

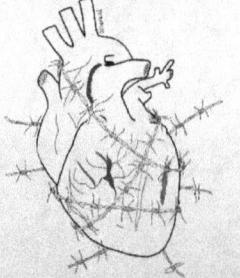

AVAILABLE DECEMBER 20TH

* REFERENCES (INTRODUCTION)

Ask Astrology. 2020. Number 0 | Numerology Meanings | Ask Astrology. [online]
Available at: <https://askastrology.com/numerology/number-0/>
[Accessed 10 August 2020].

Ask Astrology. 2020. Life Path Numbers Explained | Numerology | Ask Astrology. [online]
Available   at: <https://askastrology.com/numerology/life-path-number-meaning/#Life_Path_Number_5>
[Accessed 10 August 2020].

Affinitynumerology.com. 2020. Number 5 Meaning. [online]
Available at: <https://affinitynumerology.com/number-meanings/number-5-meaning.php>
[Accessed 10 August 2020].

Affinity Numerology. 2020. Numerology 50. [online]
Available at: <https://affinitynumerology.com/number-meanings/number-50-meaning.php>
[Accessed 10 August 2020]